YOUNG ENGINEERS

T0101091

Building Structures and Towers

by Tammy Enz

capstone®

© 2017 Heinemann-Raintree
an imprint of Capstone Global Library, LLC
Chicago, Illinois

To contact Capstone Global Library please call 800-747-4992, or visit our website www.mycapstone.com

All rights reserved. No part of this publication may be reproduced or transmitted in any form or by any means, electronic or mechanical, including photocopying, recording, taping, or any information storage and retrieval system, without permission in writing from the publisher.

Edited by Adrian Vigliano
Designed by Philippa Jenkins
Picture research by Svetlana Zhurkin
Production by Katy LaVigne
Originated by Capstone Global Library Ltd

Library of Congress Cataloging-in-Publication Data
Library of Congress Cataloging-in-Publication data is available on the Library of Congress website.

ISBN: 9781484637463 (library binding)
ISBN: 9781484637500 (pbk.)

Acknowledgments
The author and publisher are grateful to the following for permission to reproduce copyright material: Capstone Studio: Karon Dubke, cover, 8, 9, 12, 13, 16, 17, 20, 21, 24, 25, 26, 27; Shutterstock: Aha-Soft, 7, Darryl Brooks, 5, Olga Morozova, 23, pedrosala, 19, rootstock, 11, topnatthapon, 15, VOJTa Herout, 29

We would like to thank Harold Pratt for his help in the preparation of this book.

Every effort has been made to contact copyright holders of any material reproduced in this book. Any omissions will be rectified in subsequent printings if notice is given to the publisher.

All the Internet addresses (URLs) given in this book were valid at the time of going to press. However, due to the dynamic nature of the Internet, some addresses may have changed, or sites may have changed or ceased to exist since publication. While the author and publisher regret any inconvenience this may cause readers, no responsibility for any such changes can be accepted by either the author or the publisher.

Printed in the United States 5488

Table of Contents

What Is a Structure? 4
Footings and Foundations..... 6
Beams and Joists.....10
Columns.....18
X-Braces and Shear Walls.....22

Glossary 30
Find Out More.....31
Index.....32

Some words are shown in bold, **like this.** You can find out what they mean by looking in the glossary.

What Is a Structure?

Structures are all around us. Most people live in a structure. You pass lots of them when you go out. Structures and towers can be almost any size or shape. But they are built from many of the same parts. These important parts may be hidden underground, beneath floors, or inside walls. But they are the keys to holding up buildings and keeping you safe.

What kinds of structures do you see every day?

Footings and Foundations

The first step in building a structure is making a **foundation**. Without foundations, heavy buildings would sink into the soft soil beneath them. Sometimes structures sit on buried concrete columns called **piers**. Piers carry a building's weight to sturdy rock layers beneath the soil. Other structures sit on **footings**. These large slabs of concrete spread out a building's weight.

Piers are designed to support a structure's full weight.

Experiment with Footings

See how footings work in this experiment.

You will need:

- A pillow or cushion
- 2-3 cans of the same size
- A piece of thick cardboard 5 inches (13 centimeters) square

1. **Place the pillow on the floor. Set a can on its center.**

2. Stack another can on top. What happens?

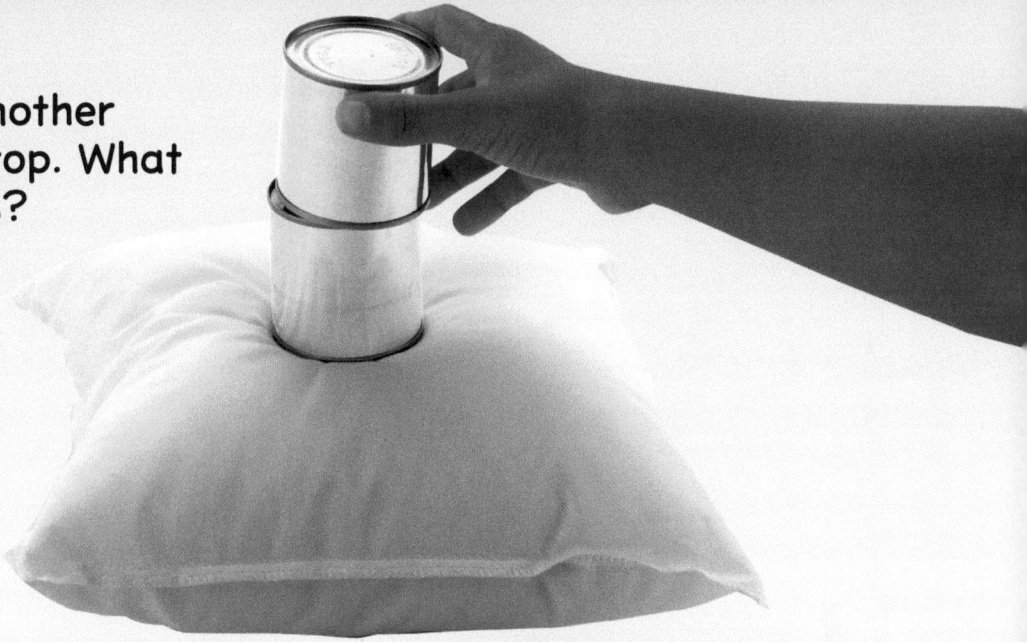

3. Remove the cans and lay the cardboard on the pillow.
4. Stack cans on the cardboard. What happens now? Do the cans sink in as far? Are they more stable?

Beams and Joists

Beams and **joists** are the structural parts of floors and roofs. They are often hidden beneath floors or above ceilings. Beams need to be strong enough to support people and things stored in buildings. Beams come in different shapes and sizes. They can be made from wood, steel, or concrete. Joists are the horizontal pieces that support a floor or ceiling. Joists are made from small pieces of steel or wood connected together.

Beams and joists form the strong skeleton of a structure.

Experiment with Beams

Beams are placed on their edges, not on their flat faces. This allows them to carry more weight. See how it works with this experiment.

You will need:

- 2 empty cereal boxes
- Tape
- 2 stacks of books
- 2-3 cans of equal size

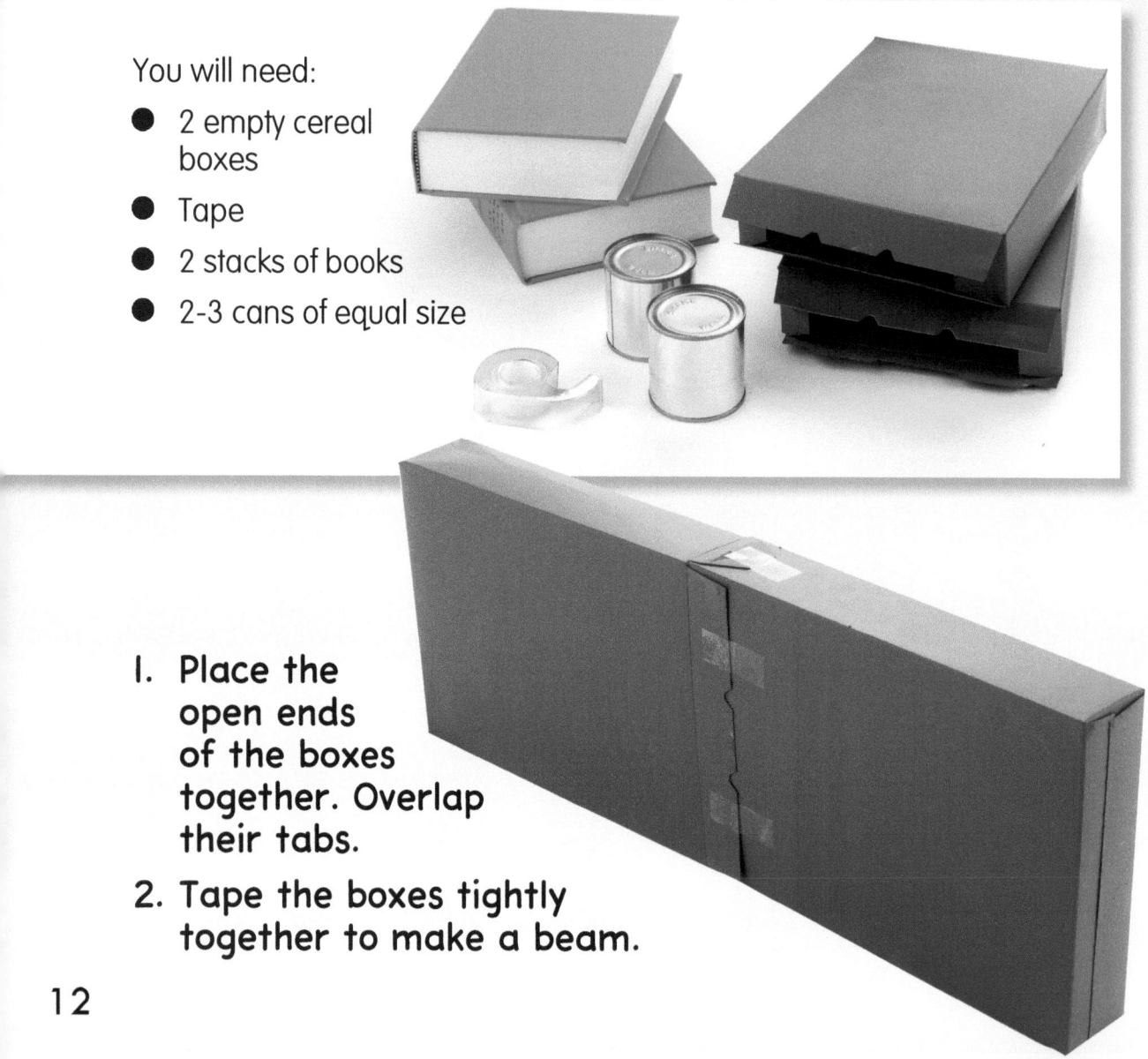

1. **Place the open ends of the boxes together. Overlap their tabs.**
2. **Tape the boxes tightly together to make a beam.**

3. Place the beam on its edge spanning the book stacks.
4. Place cans on the middle of the beam. How many cans can it hold?

5. Now place the beam on its face spanning the books.
6. How many cans can it hold now?

When loaded up, beams experience **tension** and **compression** forces. Tension forces stretch parts of beams. Compression forces squash other parts. Beams that are too compressed **buckle**. Beams that have too much tension tend to snap. Steel and wood beams stay strong when stretched and squashed. But concrete beams need to be reinforced to stay strong.

Engineers must carefully balance forces in their building designs.

Modeling a Reinforced Concrete Beam

Concrete beams break easily. But with a little help from steel reinforcing bars they remain strong. Make your own reinforced beam.

You will need:

- Pieces of polystyrene foam about 2 inch (5 cm) x 5 inch (13 cm) x 1 inch (3 cm) thick
- 2 wooden skewers

1. **Hold the ends of the foam and slowly bend it until its bottom begins to crack.**

2. Carefully slide the skewers into the foam about ¼ inch (1 cm) from the bottom of the beam. Place them about 1 inch (3 cm) apart.

3. Now bend the beam again. Do the skewers keep the beam strong?

Columns

Beams support all the weight of the things inside a building. But **columns** support that weight and the weight of the building itself and carry all of it to the foundation. Beams at each building level connect to columns. Columns can be any shape, but often have square or circle **cross sections.** Longer columns are less stable than shorter columns and buckle more easily when loaded up.

Columns help engineers create buildings with many floors.
columns

Experiment with Columns

Test out the strength of long and short columns with this experiment.

You will need:

- 3 sheets of paper
- Scissors
- Tape
- Books

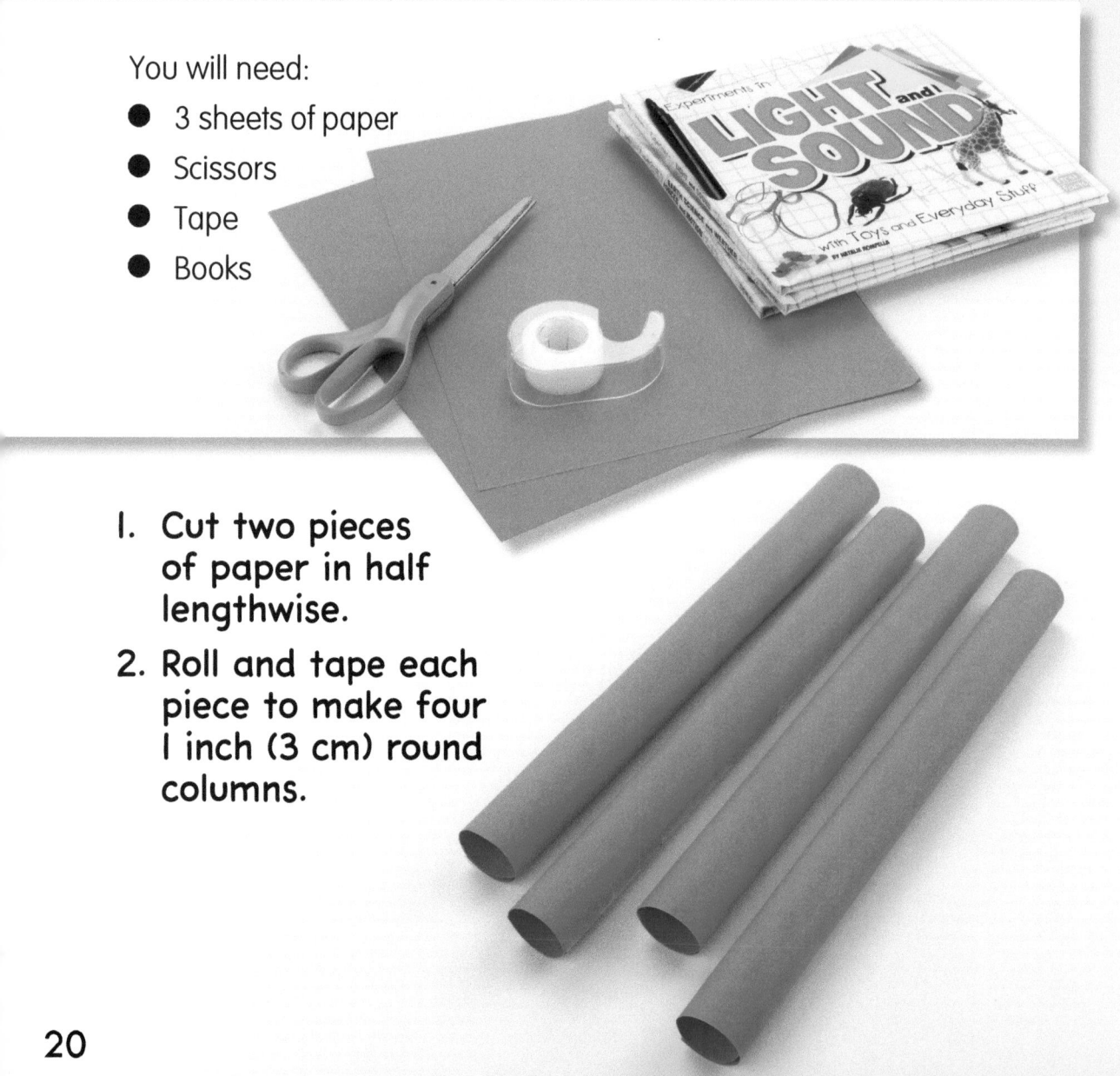

1. Cut two pieces of paper in half lengthwise.
2. Roll and tape each piece to make four 1 inch (3 cm) round columns.

3. Place a column under each corner of a book. Carefully stack on more books, one at a time. How many books can the long columns hold?

4. Cut another paper into fourths. Roll and tape each of these pieces to make four short columns.
5. Load up the short columns with books. Can they hold more?

X-Braces and Shear Walls

Beams and columns support lots of weight. But there's more to making a building or tower stand straight and tall. A **lateral,** or sideways, system prevents wind from toppling structures. **X-braces** and **shear walls** collect wind forces and carry them to the foundation. You may not see these braces but even tall glass buildings have hidden lateral systems.

X-braces are used in many different types of structures.

Experiment with Shear Walls

Shear walls are walls inside buildings that carry wind loads to the foundation. See how they work with this experiment.

You will need:

- Empty cereal box
- Tape

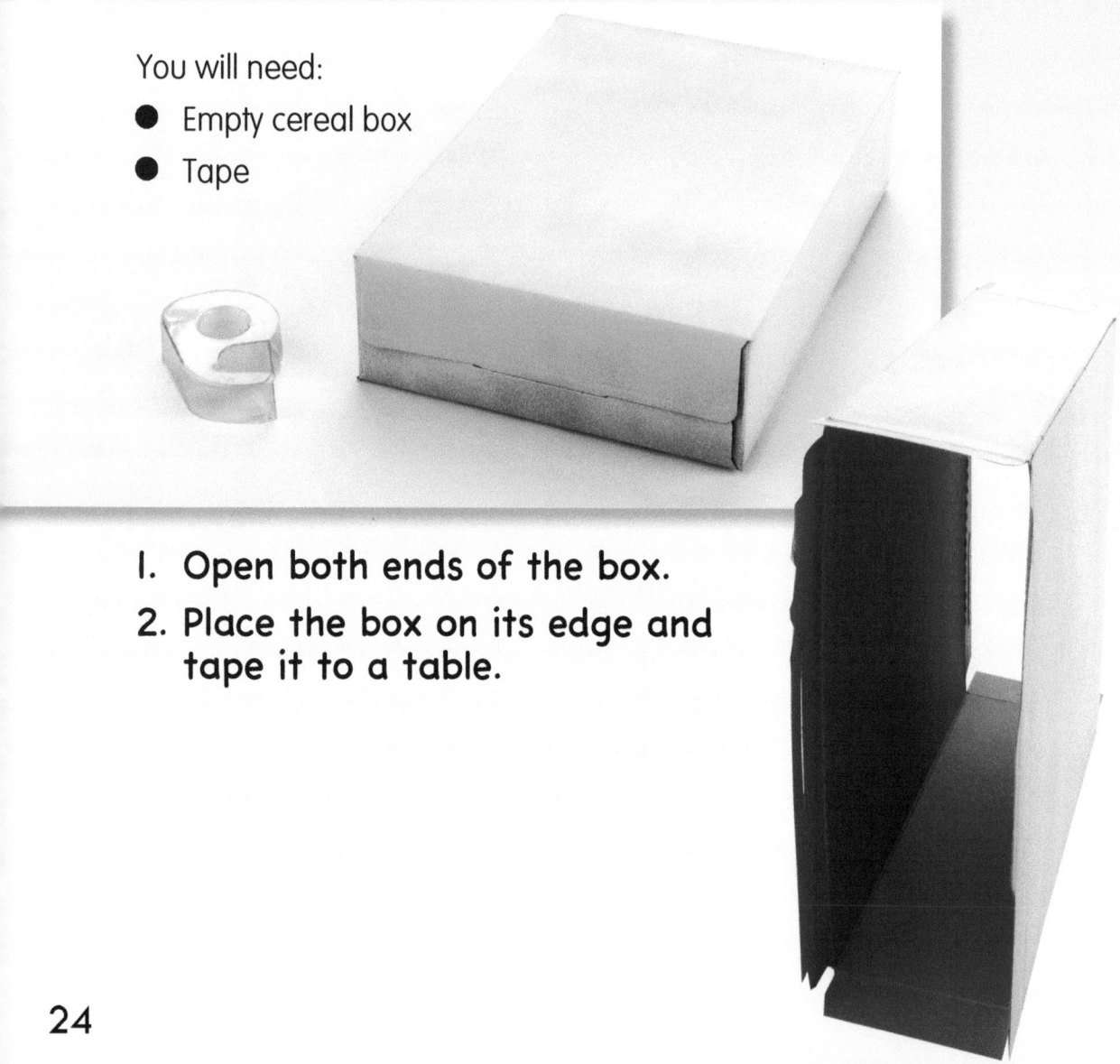

1. Open both ends of the box.
2. Place the box on its edge and tape it to a table.

3. Push against one side of the box. How easily does the box tilt?

4. Now tape the open ends of the box closed to create shear walls.
5. Push against the side as before. What happens now? Do the shear walls prevent tilting?

Build a Braced Tower

X-bracing is another way to keep buildings straight and tall when wind blows on them. See how it works with this experiment.

You will need:

- Spaghetti noodles
- Gum drops

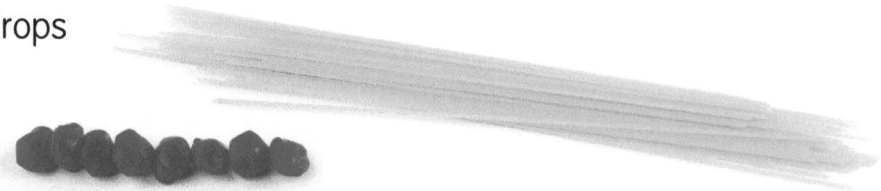

1. **Break two noodles in half. Use gum drops to connect the pieces into a square.**
2. **Repeat Step 1 to make another square.**

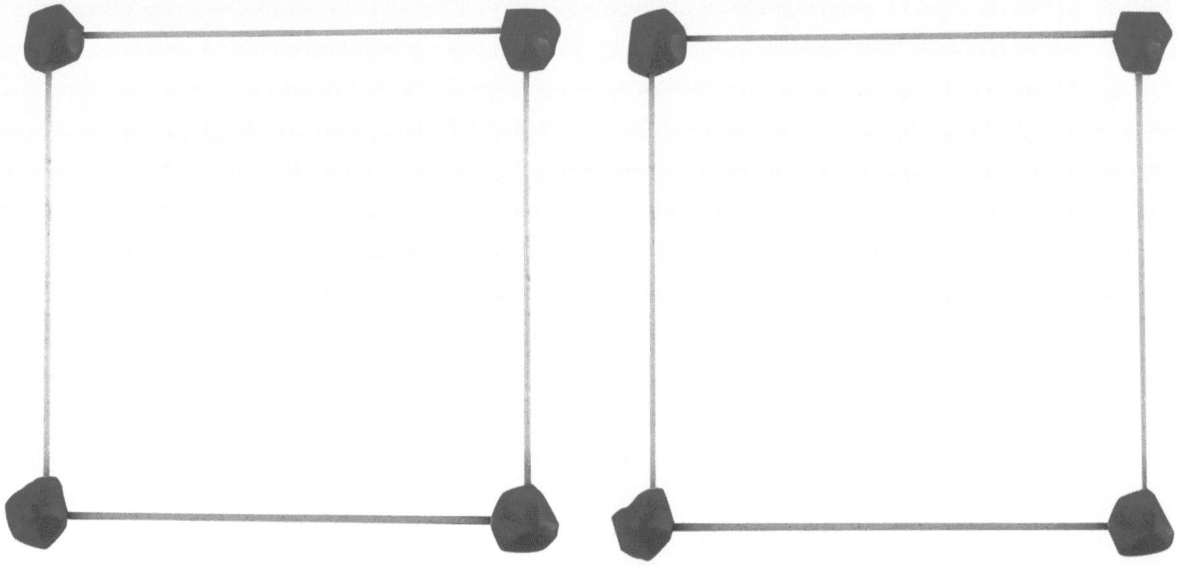

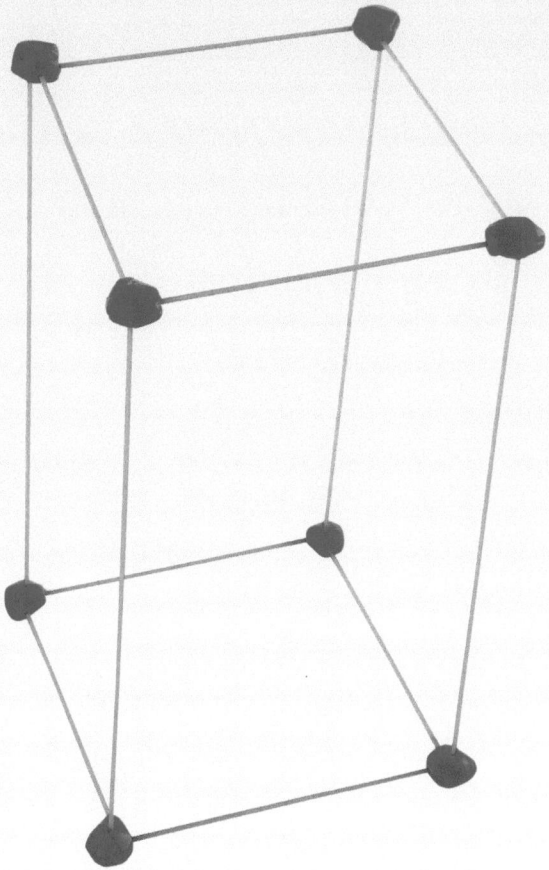

3. Break a 1 inch (3 cm) piece off four more noodles.
4. Use these long noodles as columns to connect the squares into a tower.
5. Push sideways on the top of the tower. What happens?

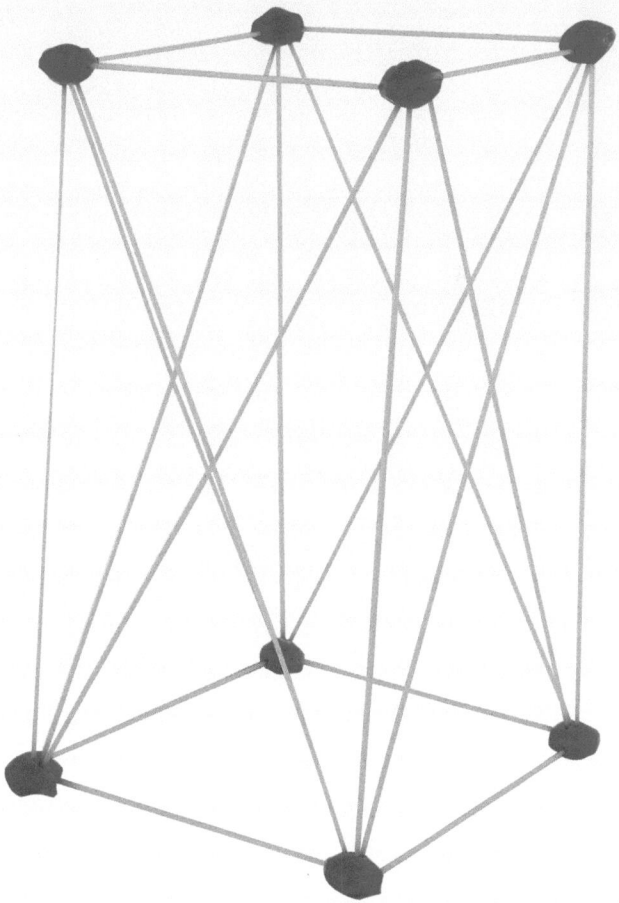

6. Add noodle x's across each side of the tower. Now what happens when you push sideways?

Structures and towers are amazing to look at. But there's more to them than meets the eye. You know about their important parts. They all need foundations. They also need beams and columns to carry the people and things inside them. Just as important are braces and walls to keep them tall and straight when wind blows.

Engineers work hard each day to design the next great building.

Glossary

beam—a support for floors and roofs
buckle—to bend under force
column—an upright support pillar
compression—a force that squishes
cross section—the shape you see when you cut through something
footing—wide concrete slab under a building column
foundation—support at the bottom of a building
joist—beam made from short pieces of steel or wood supporting part of the structure of a building; horizontal piece that supports a floor or ceiling
lateral—sideways
pier—an underground support column
reinforcing—making stronger
shear wall—wall designed to resist wind forces
structure—the load carrying parts of a building
tension—a pulling force
X-brace—crossing members that resist wind forces

Find Out More

Books

Ames, Lee J. *Draw 50 Buildings and Other Structures.* New York: Watson-Guptill Publications, 2013.

Beck, Barbara. *The Future Architect's Handbook.* Atglen, Pa.: Schiffer Publishing, Ltd., 2014.

Graham, Ian. *Great Building Designs 1900–Today.* Chicago: Heinemann Raintree, 2016.

Internet sites

Facthound offers a safe, fun way to find Internet sites related to this book. All of the sites on Facthound have been researched by our staff.

Here's all you do:
Visit *www.facthound.com*
Type in this code: 9781484637463

Index

beams, 10, 12, 13, 14, 16, 17, 18, 28

columns, 6, 18, 20, 21, 22, 27, 28
compression, 14
concrete, 6, 10, 14, 16
cross sections, 18

footings, 6, 8
foundations, 6, 18, 22, 24, 28

joists, 10

piers, 6

rock layers, 6

tension, 14

walls, 4, 22, 24, 25, 28
weight, 6, 12, 18, 22
wind, 22, 24, 26, 28

X-braces, 22